A

Gnostic Prayer Book

Collected Prayers, Mantras,

and Meditations

Practical Techniques to Develop the Soul

Surekha Minati Keerthana

GLORIAN

A Gnostic Prayer Book
A Glorian Book / 2014

© 2014 Glorian Publishing

Print ISBN: 978-1-934206-48-5
Ebook ISBN: 978-1-934206-60-7

Glorian Publishing is a non-profit
organization. All proceeds go to further
the distribution of these books. For more
information, visit gnosticteachings.org.

Contents

If there is to be peace in the world,
There must be peace in the nations.

If there is to be peace in the nations,
There must be peace in the cities.

If there is to be peace in the cities,
There must be peace between neighbors.

If there is to be peace between neighbors,
There must be peace in the home.

If there is to be peace in the home,
There must be peace in the heart.

- Lao-Tzu

"The fragrance of sandalwood and rosebay does not
travel far, but the fragrance of virtue rises to the heavens."
- Buddha Shakyamuni, from The Dhammapada

Foreword

This book is not intended to be a Gnostic prayer book in the historical sense, but rather Gnosticism in the practical sense, for the modern aspiring Gnostic student. While many in these times associate the word Gnosis with a collection of texts found in the deserts of the Middle East (such as the Nag Hammdhi texts or the Dead Sea Scrolls), or with long-lost groups of spiritual seekers (like the Essenes), the truth is that those writings and groups were but one fraction of a much older, more widespread movement, one that cannot be tracked by physical evidence alone: it can only be truly known through awakened, conscious experience—not only here in the physical world, but also in the internal worlds, by means of techniques such as meditation, dream yoga, and more.

The Greek word **Gnosis** refers to the knowledge acquired through the experience of the awakened consciousness, as opposed to knowledge that we are told or might believe. Genuine Gnosis is the knowledge universal to all humanity that frees the consciousness from suffering. Gnosis—by whatever name in history or culture—is conscious, experiential knowledge, not merely intellectual or conceptual knowledge, belief or theory. The Gnostic student seeks to acquire their own direct experience of the light (the truth) by means of awakening the consciousness and eliminating obscurations to perception. The method to accomplish this task has been called:

Gnosis: (Greek) knowledge

Jnana: (Sanskrit) knowledge

Daath: (Hebrew) knowledge

Dharma: (Sanskrit) righteousness, law, truth, teaching

Torah: (Hebrew) teaching, instruction, law

...and many other names. By comparing all of these ancient teachings, we can see that all religious forms have in their heart a science of *Gnosticism:* a method to arrive at personal knowledge of the truth.

Messengers arrive from time to time to clarify the knowledge for us: messengers such as Buddha, Jesus, Mohammed, Quetzalcoatl, Krishna, Moses, Fu Xi, Samael Aun Weor, and many others: all of them taught Gnosis, but according to the needs of the time and place. That is why within this book you will find a true collection of Gnostic prayers—prayers from many religions, philosophies, teachers, and masters.

"O gods! All your names and forms are to be revered, saluted, and adored." - Rig Veda X, 63, 2

"Religions are different roads converging upon the same point. What does it matter that we take different roads so long as we reach the same goal." - Mahatma Gandhi

"Life is short. Time is fleeting. Realize the Self. Purity of the heart is the gateway to God. Aspire. Renounce. Meditate. Be good; do good. Be kind; be compassionate. Inquire, know Thyself." - Swami Sivananda

Christ in the Garden of Gethsemane,
by Heinrich Hofmann (1890)

Introduction

> *"...When you pray, go into your room, close the door and pray to your Father, who is unseen. Then your Father, who sees what is done in secret, will reward you."* - Jesus, Matthew 6:6

Prayer nourishes our lives. It is the way we can speak to God, our Being, Allah, Jehovah Elohim, Ahura Mazda, Buddha, Brahma, the Creator. It is our way of connecting to a force superior to ourselves so that we can ask for guidance, advice, wisdom, protection, strength, health, security, and love. "God Wants to Talk to You," it says on my computer desktop. It reminds me that I need to go within to get in touch with my Being, because He/She wants to teach me something. It reminds me that I am a spiritual being living in a physical world. It reminds me that I am one with everything around me for we all share the same Father above and Mother Earth below.

Many people wonder, "Am I praying correctly? Am I doing this right?" All that is needed in order to pray is sincerity within our supplication, love within our heart, and a longing to become closer with the Divine so that we can hear the whispers of teachings that He longs to give us. Praying mechanically is useless. Our consciousness must be alert, here and now, in order to be able to grasp the guidance from within. As Samael Aun Weor, a great master, said,

"When the mind has achieved absolute calm and silence, it can concentrate on the inner Self. This concentration is done with the help of prayer. Pray to your inner Self. Try to converse with your inner Self. Remember that praying is conversing with God. You can pray without formulae; in other words, talk to God, tell Him what your heart feels, with infinite love."

Speaking sincerely from our heart is praying. Listening sincerely to our heart is praying. Communion with the intelligence that is sacred within us is the goal of prayer.

True prayer is spontaneous, emotional, energetic, never dull, mechanical, nor repeated automatically. True prayer is communication, interaction, energy in motion; it is the very heart of our Being meeting itself, and from that convergence, light emerges.

Gnosis is conscious, experiential knowledge and sincere prayer results in gnosis, which is light for the soul. Prayer is also a sacred act of listening, listening to the inner guidance of our divine Being.

"God speaks in the silence of the heart. Listening is the beginning of prayer." - Mother Teresa

The words we use, the prayers we utter, are a way to speak our own heart's longing of our inner Being.

"Prayer is not asking. It is a longing of the soul. It is daily admission of one's weakness. It is better in prayer to have a heart without words than words without a heart." - Mahatma Gandhi

"Really, it is necessary to learn how to pray scientifically; the one who learns to intelligently combine prayer with meditation will obtain marvelous objective results. But it is urgent to comprehend that there are different prayers and that their results are different. There are prayers which are accompanied by petitions, but not all prayers are accompanied by petitions. There are very ancient prayers which are authentic recapitulations of cosmic events and we can experience their entire content if we meditate on each word, on each phrase, with true cognizant devotion." - Samael Aun Weor

Ultimately, prayer is a process that helps us to develop who we truly are. In order to achieve this, we must learn to be patient with ourselves and with the process of self-realization for this is the greatest work we will ever undergo.

"The greatest prayer is patience." - Buddha

"Seek assistance through patience and prayer, and most surely it is

a hard thing except for the humble ones." - Quran, The Cow 2.45

We must truly trust in our inner Being. Our God within knows much better than we do what it is we truly need to achieve this perfect union. That is, when we pray, we should put our longings into the hands of our Innermost. If we do this, we have to let go of those longings. If we are still holding on to what we want, what we expect, what we desire, we have not truly placed them into the hands of the Divine. Put them into the hands of your Innermost, and let them go.

"Our prayers should be for blessings in general, for God knows best what is good for us." - Socrates

We hope that the prayers included in this book will help open your heart and Inner Mind and give you the protection and guidance you need from the Divinity you long to know directly.

You can have confidence in these prayers. They have been passed on to us from the most elevated masters of our most venerable traditions. Each prayer has been proven effective. Use them wisely, consciously, and with genuine faith in your Innermost. Prayer is the thread that links us to our Divine. Find your words. Pray them. Listen. Be patient. And keep praying…

"May you be filled with loving kindness. May you be well. May you be peaceful and at ease. May you be happy."
- Ancient Tibetan Buddhist Blessing

Everyday Prayers

There are so many wonderful, powerful, majestic prayers in the world. Here is a collection of everyday prayers that you could use in your spiritual practice.

Prayer of the Lord (Pater Noster)

"Our Father, who art in heaven,
  hallowed be Thy name.

"Thy kingdom come.

"Thy will be done on earth,
  as it is in heaven.

"Give us this day our daily bread,
  and forgive us our trespasses, as we
  forgive those who trespass against us.

"And lead us not into temptation,
  but deliver us from evil.

"For Thine is the kingdom, the power,
  and the glory forever. Amen."

Among all of the ritual prayers, the most powerful is the Pater Noster (Prayer of the Lord). This is a magical prayer of immense power. Samael Aun Weor said, "The heart chakra develops with meditation and the most profound prayer. We advise you to pray the Our Father. A well-prayed Our Father is equivalent to one hour of meditation; pray, therefore, the Our Father for one hour. To pray is to converse with God. Hence, immerse yourself into a very profound slumber state and meditate very deeply, thus, converse mentally with God. Each phrase of the Our Father is a complete formula in order to talk to Him. So, while in a slumber state, meditate on the contents of each phrase, this is how the Father, Who is in secret, can be seen and heard. This is how the heart chakra awakens."

The Gayatri Mantra

The Gayatri Mantra has both the power of mantra and of prayer. It is a universal prayer, which asks for a clear intellect so that the truth may be reflected without distortion. Chanting it with humility, reverence, faith and love is more important than mechanical repetition.

Because the prayer is in Sanskrit, the meaning does not translate easily to English. Even the name of the prayer is very powerful: *Gayatri* comes from:

gaya: vital energies
trayate: deliver, liberate, preserve

Thus, this prayer is a sacred method for transforming energy.

Gayatri, the feminine form of Brahma

There are many "versions" of this prayer, whether shorter or longer. This one is perhaps the most widely known:

"Om Buhr, Bhuva, Swaha

"Om Tat Savitur Varenyam

"Bhargo Devasya Dheemahi

"Dhiyo Yonaha Prachodayat."

Which means, "We meditate on the glory of the Creator; Who has created the universe; Who is worthy of worship; Who is the embodiment of knowledge and light; Who is the remover of sin and ignorance; May He open our hearts and enlighten our minds."

Peace Prayer of St. Francis

The Peace Prayer of Saint Francis is attributed to the saint who was born at Assisi, but does not appear in any of his known writings. It first appeared around the year 1915 AD.

After a care free youth, St. Francis turned his back on inherited wealth and committed himself to God. He lived a very simple life of poverty and humbleness. He loved God's creatures— birds and beasts—and treated them as brothers and sisters, thus he gained a reputation of being the friend of animals. He established the rule of St. Francis, which exists today as the Order of St. Francis, or the Franciscans.

"Lord, make me an instrument
  of your peace,

"Where there is hatred,
  let me sow love;
  where there is injury, pardon;
  where there is doubt, faith;

where there is despair, hope;
where there is darkness, light;
where there is sadness, joy;

"O Divine Master, grant that I may not
so much seek to be consoled as to
console;
to be understood as to understand;
to be loved as to love.

"For it is in giving that we receive;
it is in pardoning that we are
pardoned; and it is in dying that
we are born to eternal life."

Shema

The Shema can be found in the Jewish prayer book (Siddur) and is considered one of the most important prayers in Judaism. It is usually recited in the morning and the evening. Most of the prayers found in this book speak to God, but not the Shema; it speaks to the Jewish people, teaching them how to behave towards God and one another.

The complete Shema is actually more than just the famous six words *Shema Yisrael, Adonai eloheinu, Adonai echad;* it is composed of three parts linked together into a unity: Deuteronomy 6:4-9, Deuteronomy 11:13-21, and Numbers 15:37-41. Here is the first part, known as Shema.

"Hear, O Israel: Jehovah
Elohim is one Jehovah:

"And thou shalt love Jehovah Elohim
with all thine heart, and with all
thy soul, and with all thy might.

"And these words, which I command
thee this day, shall be in thine heart:

"And thou shalt teach them diligently
unto thy children, and shalt talk
of them when thou sittest in thine
house, and when thou walkest

by the way, and when thou liest down, and when thou risest up.

"And thou shalt bind them for a sign upon thine hand, and they shall be as frontlets between thine eyes.

"And thou shalt write them upon the posts of thy house, and on thy gates."

Hail, Mary

Around the world and throughout history, the Divine Mother has been known by many names. She was known as Tonantzin amongst the Aztecs, as Diana among the Greeks, and as Isis to the Egyptians. For the Christians, the Divine Mother is represented by Mary.

Mary, the Christian symbol of the Divine Mother

To pray to God, we must understand that God has a masculine force and a feminine force: the goddess, the Divine Mother. God is male-female. This prayer is to our Divine Mother.

The physical mother of Master Jesus of Nazareth, the Rabbi from Galilee, was Mary, a great female master, the incarnation of a goddess related with the elements of nature. Two thousand years ago, when Christianity began, she took the responsibility of representing the Divine Mother in Christianity. Being a priestess of the temple of Israel, she received that honor. That is why we call her Mary, "the mother of God." We understand very well that the Divine Mother Mary, the mother of God, has no form, because She is beyond form. But the initiate Mary, the mother of Jesus who came two thousand years ago, is a master who represents the Divine Mother above, just as Master Jesus represents Christ. Christ is universal. The Divine Mother is universal and is formless, ineffable, but is represented by Mary, the mother of Jesus.

"Hail, Mary, full of grace, the Lord is with thee.

"Blessed art thou amongst women, and blessed is the fruit of thy womb, Yeshua.

"Holy Mary, Mother of God, pray
  for us, who have the sinning
  'I,' now and at the hour of the
  death of our defects. Amen."

*"Pray and meditate intensely. The Divine
Mother teaches her children. Prayer must be
performed by combining meditation with the
sleepy state. Then, as in a vision of a dream,
illumination emerges. The Divine Mother
comes to the devotee in order to instruct
them in the great mysteries."* - Samael Aun Weor

Prayer to the Divine Mother

"Oh Divine Mother, I am all Yours.

"You are my only refuge and support.

"Protect me, guide me,
  have pity on me."

*"God does not have any form. God is co-
essential to the abstract absolute space. God
is that... that... that. God has two aspects,
wisdom and love. As wisdom, God is the
Father; as love, God is the Mother. [...] The
Cosmic Mother has no form, but will take on
any form in order to answer the supplicant.
She can present herself in the form of Isis,*

Rhea, Cybele, Tonantzin, Mary, etc. [...] The Divine Mother is not a woman, nor is she an individual. She is in fact an unknown substance. God the Mother is love. God the Mother adores us and loves us tremendously." - Samael Aun Weor, The Yellow Book

The Divine Mother takes whatever form is needed.

Aztec Prayer to the Divine Mother

Ancient wisdom teaches that each of us has a Divine Mother, and She can take any form, for She is the origin of all forms. Here, she is called by one of Her Aztec names, Tonantzin. Meditate upon Her before falling asleep. Start your dreaming process by repeating daily with great faith the following prayer:

"Tonantzin, Teteoinan!

"My Mother, come to me, come to me!"

According to Tantric science, if the Gnostic persists with this practice, sooner or later an Initiator Element will come forth from the changing and formless expressions of his dreams. Read *Dream Yoga* by Samael Aun Weor.

Zoroastrian Prayer

Zarathushtra or Zoroaster was an ancient Iranian prophet and philosopher. He was the founder of the pre-Islamic religion Zoroastrianism, which is synonymous with Mazdaism, the worship of Ahura Mazda (Christ). At present, most of the Zoroastrians or Parsis are living in India. Friedrich Nietzsche fictionalized Zarathustra's story in his book *Thus Spoke Zarathustra.*

"Do what thy God wilt fully will; I adjust my will to thy will, Ahura Mazda.

"Let me will what thou willest me to will. Work thy will in me. I will accept thy will as law and submit to it. My lip-loyalty to thee does not mean anything. It counts for nothing. Doing thy will, living according to thy will, is everything. I will do all that thou willest me to do. I will keep thy commandments with all my will. I will conform my life to thy will. Every day in my life, I will do what is pleasing to thee and refrain from doing what is displeasing to thee. Help me to restrain my self-will.

"Infallible is thy divine will. What thou dost win is always good, for thou, the Sovereign Lord of mankind without a second, art All-good thyself. Thou wert the same yesterday. Thou art the same today and thou will be the same for ever. The creation came into being with thy will. I see thy designing will and ordaining hand in everything.

"Things always come about as thou dost will. What thou doest is always the best in the end. Thou dost work thy will upon me. Do unto me as thou willest. Inflame my will with love for thee. I will do all that thou willest me to do. Let me see the right, let me understand the right, and let me have the will to do the right.

"With my hands uplifted, my head bent low, I will sink on my knees and bow to thy will. I will think and speak and do as thou wouldst have me to do. Enlighten me with thy will, that I may make it known all around me.

"My life is built around thee. Let thy will dominate my will. I will not live my life as I will, but as thou dost will. Faithfully will I comply with thy will. Let thy will govern my will. Let my will be merged in thy will and become one with it. With the fullness of my heart I will always do thy will, Ahura Mazda."

Apostles' Creed

The Apostle's Creed or Symbolum Apostolorum summarizes the teachings of the Apostles of Jesus, and is recited in many Christian traditions.

Samael Aun Weor advises to recite the "Pater Noster" or the "Prayer of the Lord" (Our Father) the "Hail, Mary" and the "Apostle's Creed," which are very ancient Gnostic prayers. Two of these prayers are in his book entitled *The Virgin of Carmel.*

"I believe in God, the Father almighty, creator of heaven and earth, and in Jesus Christ, His only Son, Our Lord who was conceived by the Holy Spirit, born of the Virgin Mary, suffered under Pontius Pilate, was crucified, died, and was buried. He descended into hell. The third day He rose again from the dead.

"He ascended into heaven, and sitteth at the right hand of God the Father almighty. From thence He shall come to judge the living and the dead.

"I believe in the Holy Spirit, the holy Gnostic Church, the Communion

of Saints, the forgiveness of sins,
the resurrection of the body,
and life everlasting. Amen."

Universal Prayer of Gurudev Swami Sivananda

Swami Sivananda was one of the greatest Yoga masters as well as a Hindu spiritual teacher. He promoted the philosophy of Yoga and Vedanta taught in the Vedas, the most ancient scriptures of India.

"O adorable Lord of mercy and love!

"Salutations and prostrations unto Thee!

"Thou art omnipresent, omnipotent and omniscient!

"Thou Art Sat-Chit-Ananda (Existence-Knowledge-Bliss)!

"Thou art the Indweller of all beings!

"Grant us an understanding heart,

"Equal vision, balanced mind,

"Faith, devotion and wisdom!

"Grant us inner spiritual
strength to resist temptations
and to control the mind!

"Free us from egoism, lust, greed,
anger, jealousy and hatred!

"Fill our hearts with divine virtues!

"Let us behold Thee in all
these names and forms!

"Let us serve Thee in all these
names and forms!

"Let us ever remember Thee!

"Let us ever sing Thy glories!

"Let Thy Name be ever on our lips!

"Let us abide in Thee
forever and ever!"

A Prayer by Shantideva

This is a prayer by Shantideva, a renowned
Indian Buddhist master from the eighth century
who wrote *The Bodhisattva's Way of Living
(Bodhicharyavatara).*

"May all beings everywhere, plagued
 by sufferings of body and mind,
 obtain an ocean of happiness
 and joy by virtue of my merits.

"May no living creature suffer, commit
 evil, or ever fall ill.May no one be
 afraid or belittled, with a mind
 weighed down by depression.

"May the blind see forms and the
 deaf hear sounds, may those
 whose bodies are worn with toil
 be restored on finding repose.

"May the naked find clothing, the
 hungry find food; may the thirsty
 find water and delicious drinks.

"May the poor find wealth, those
 weak with sorrow find joy; may
 the forlorn find hope, constant
 happiness, and prosperity.

"May there be timely rains and
 bountiful harvests; may all
 medicines be effective and
 wholesome prayers bear fruit.

"May all who are sick and ill quickly
be freed from their ailments.
Whatever diseases there are in the
world, may they never occur again.

"May the frightened cease to be afraid
and those bound be freed; may
the powerless find power, and may
people think of benefiting each other.

"For as long as space remains, for
as long as sentient beings remain,
until then may I too remain to
dispel the miseries of the world."

*Mahayana Buddhists around the world recite
daily their aspiration to serve others.*

Jehovah God

This prayer is used in order to ask for blessings for your entire family.

"In the name of Jehovah God, Christ Jesus, pray for my brethren, my father, my mother, my children, my nephews, my nieces, and all my friends who are good hearted, by my glory to God, the Father, and the Holy Spirit."

Morning Prayer

Every morning before getting out of bed, say the following Morning Prayer filled with force and energy:

"We are strong. We are rich. We are filled with luck and harmony. Om, Om, Om."

"Recite this simple prayer and you will see that you are prosperous in everything. Have great devotion in this prayer. Have faith. It is necessary to abandon the bad habit of talking about ourselves at every moment. It

is urgent to employ the Word to strengthen and encourage the good qualities of our fellowman. The Gnostic student should abandon the extremely bad habit of naming himself and telling the story of his life at every moment. The man or woman who only talks of himself or herself becomes unbearable. Persons like this fall into misery because people become tired of them. Never say, "I." Always say, "we." The term "we" has more cosmic power. The term "I" is egotistical and tires all those who come in contact with us. The "I" is egotistical. The "I" should be dissolved. The "I" is a creator of conflicts and problems. Always repeat: "we, we, we…" - Samael Aun Weor

Evening Prayer and Exercise

In front of a mirror, contemplate your face closely. Then pray as follows:

"My Soul, you should succeed. My Soul, you should overcome Satan.

"My Soul, take over my mind, my sentiments, my life. You should keep the Guardian of the Threshold far away from me. You should overcome him. You should take power over me totally. Amen. Amen. Amen."

Say this prayer seven times and then observe in the mirror your eyes, your pupils, the center of your pupils, the retina of your eyes. Imagine them charged with light, strength and power. It is necessary that you try to mentally penetrate the interior of your eyes reflected in the mirror. It is necessary for you to try and see with your imagination, the center of those reflected eyes, the beauty of your soul. It is necessary for you to exclaim: "Oh my soul, I want to see you, I want to see you, I want to see you." Intensely persevere, daily, with this exercise. Do your exercise every night before going to sleep. With this exercise you will develop clairvoyance. Practice for ten minutes daily.

"The Guardian of the Threshold is our Satan... our internal beast, the source of all of our animal passions and brutal appetites..." - Samael Aun Weor, The Revolution of Beelzebub

A Prayer Before Death

This prayer by the fourteenth century Tibetan Nyingma Master Longchenpa Rabjampa prepares the consciousness to remain vigilant as it passes through the bardo, a Tibetan word that describes the interval between death and the next rebirth.

"When my time has come and
impermanence and death
have caught up with me,

"When the breath ceases, and the body
and mind go their separate ways,

"May I not experience delusion,
attachment, and clinging,

"But remain in the natural
state of ultimate reality."

Prayers Before Meals

Food is more than just a means of bodily nourishment. It influences our mental, spiritual, and emotional development. Therefore, we should take great care in what we put into our bodies.

How we eat is also important. In order to extract all of the energy of the food, we can mentally vocalize the mantra **Krim** (pronounced *krrrrreeeemmmm*, with a rolled r if possible, and the e as in tree). This energy will then not only feed our physical body but our internal bodies as well. When we eat, we must remember God and pronounce the mantra Krim so that the energy can nourish us spiritually.

Grace

When we sit down to eat our meals, God should be remembered and thanked. With this traditional Christian prayer, or Grace, we can focus on the blessings, on the gift of food that God has provided us. We should eat with gratitude, mindfulness, and be present in order to fully benefit from the food.

"Bless us, O Lord, and these your gifts, which we are about to receive from your goodness through Christ our Lord. Amen."

Hindu Prayer Before a Meal

"Brahmarpanam brahma havir brahmagnau brahmanaahutam brahmaiva tena gantavyam brahma-karma-samadhina."

Quoted from Bhagavad-gita 4:24, this prayer means: "Brahman is offering Brahman through Brahman for the sake of Brahman," a beautiful teaching about the law of reciprocal nourishment.

Tibetan Prayer Before a Meal

"I offer the essence of this food to the Three Precious Jewels: the Precious Buddha, the Precious Dharma, the Precious Sangha. Please bless this food that we may take it as a medicine, with our minds free from attachment and desire. May it nourish our bodies so that we can work for the benefit of all sentient beings."

Muslim Prayers for Meals

Prayer before a meal:

"Bismillahi wa 'ala baraka-tillah."

Meaning: "By Allah's name and blessings (do we eat)."

Prayer after a meal:

"Alham do lillah hilla-thee at Amana wa saquana waja 'alana minal Muslimeen."

Meaning: "Thank you, Allah, for feeding us and making us amongst the believers."

Gokan-no-ge

The "Five Reflections" or "Five Remembrances" are chanted before a meal in the Zen Buddhist tradition.

"First, let us reflect on our own
work and the effort of those who
have brought us this food.

"Second, let us be aware of the quality
of our deeds as we receive this meal.

"Third, what is most essential
is the practice of mindfulness,
which helps us to transcend
greed, anger, and delusion.

"Fourth, we appreciate this
food which sustains the good
health of our body and mind.

"Fifth, in order to continue our practice
for all beings we accept this offering."

Invocations

An invocation is a call for aid or support. Memorize these invocations so that they will immediately be available for use in moments of need.

Song of the Angel Aroch

The angel Aroch taught this conjuration to Samael Aun Weor for protection against negative forces. It should be sung.

"Belilin... Belilin... Belilin...

"Amphora of salvation...

"I would like to be next to you...

"Materialism has no power over me...

"Belilin... Belilin... Belilin..."

Katha Upanishad (Invocation)

"Om Saha Naavavatu

"Saha Nau Bhunaktu

"Saha Veeryam Karavaavahai

"Tejasvinaa Vadheetamastu

"Maa Vidvishaa Vahai

"Om Shantih, Shantih, Shantih."

Meaning: "Om. May He protect us both. May He nourish us both. May we be given strength. May spiritual knowledge shine before us. May we never oppose one another. Om. Peace! Peace! Peace!"

Invocation

In the internal worlds (other dimensions) is the possibility of consciously projecting ourselves in the Astral Body. This capacity must be established as a habit that can be exercised voluntarily at any given moment and under any circumstance, whether alone or before witnesses. When you start recognizing that you are sleeping, that is the first step to awaken. If you realize that you are not awake, then it is a sign that you want to awaken; then, do super efforts to awaken. Use the mantra **Om Tat Sat Om** to activate your pineal gland, which is the only gland related with the Being. When we are there, our Monad is helping us, sending us a lot of force to pull us because we are part of Him.

While awakened in the internal worlds, use this invocation to call upon any positive being, or to clarify the true identity of any who appear before you.

"In the name of Christ, by the majesty of Christ, by the power of Christ!"

Invocation of Solomon

The great magician and Kabbalist Solomon, son of David and King of Israel, gave this powerful gift to humanity. In order to understand the names written in this prayer, one must study Kabbalah, since in order to actualize the power of this prayer, one must be an authentic Kabbalist; that is, one must be acquiring cognizance—conscious experience—of the ten Sephiroth of the Tree of Life. Nevertheless, since this prayer calls upon many important names of God, it can be used in order to call for immediate assistance, guidance, and protection.

"Powers of the Kingdom, be ye under
my left foot and in my right hand!

"Glory and Eternity, take me by
the two shoulders and direct
me in the paths of victory!

"Mercy and Justice, be ye the
equilibrium and splendor of my life!

"Intelligence and Wisdom, crown me!

"Spirits of Malkuth, lead me betwixt
the two pillars upon which rests
the whole edifice of the temple!

"Angels of Netzach and Hod, establish
me upon the cubic stone of Yesod!

"Oh Gedulael! Oh Geburael!
Oh Tiphereth!

"Binael, be my love!

"Ruach Chokmael, be thou my light!

"Be that which thou art and
thou shalt be, O Ketheriel!

"Ishim, assist me in the name of Shaddai!

"Cherubim, be my strength
in the name of Adonai!

"Beni-Elohim, be my brethren
in the name of the Son, and by
the powers of Sabbaoth!

"Elohim, do battle for me in the
name of Tetragrammaton!

"Melachim, protect me in the
name of Yod Hei Vav Hei!

"Seraphim, cleanse my love
in the name of Eloah!

"Hasmalim, enlighten me with the
splendors of Elohim and Shekinah!

"Aralim, act!

"Orphanim, revolve and shine!

"Hajoth ha Kadosh, cry,
speak, roar, bellow!

"Kadosh, Kadosh, Kadosh!

"Shaddai, Adonai, Yod-Havah,

"Eheieh Asher Eheieh!

"Hallelu-jah, Hallelu-jah, Hallelu-jah,

"Amen. Amen. Amen."

Invocations of the Divine Mother

Samael Aun Weor wrote: "This prayer with its mantras can be utilized in Sexual Magic. This prayer with its mantras is an omnipotent clue in order to meditate upon our Divine Mother. The Master Huiracocha (Dr. Krumm-Heller) stated the following in his *Rosicrucian Novel:* 'When the man joins the woman in the secret act, he becomes a god since in that moment he converts himself into a Creator. Seers state that in those precise moments of love, the two beings are seen enveloped by a brilliant burst of light; they are enveloped by the most subtle and potent forces in nature. If man and woman knew how to withdraw without the spasm and retain that vibration, then they can operate with it as a magician in order to purify themselves and obtain everything. However, if they do not know how to retain that light, it will withdraw from them in order to set out into the universal currents, yet leaving behind the open doors so that evil can introduce itself to them. Then love is converted into hatred; their illusion is followed by deception.'

"With the mantric prayer that we have taught in this lesson, we retain that brilliant cosmic light that envelops the human couple in that supreme moment of love with the condition of avoiding, by all means, the ejaculation of the Ens Seminis. The mantras of this invocation have the power of transmuting the creative energies into light and fire. The bachelor and bachelorettes can also transmute and sublimate their sexual energies and carry them to the heart with this prayer and these mantras. You must know that in the temple of the heart, the creative energies are mixed with the forces of Christ and thereafter they elevate to the superior worlds. The Inner Christ lives in the heart temple. The cross of initiation is received in the heart temple. This mantric prayer is also a formula of priestly power that the magician utilizes in his practices of internal meditation in order to arrive at the feet of his Divine Mother. If the meditation is perfect, your adorable Mother will hear your call and she will come to you; then you can converse with her about ineffable, paradisiacal things. She is Devi Kundalini; She is the Empress of the Tarot. The Divine Mother always listens to her devotees."

To learn more, read *The Revolution of Beelzebub* and *The Perfect Matrimony* by Samael Aun Weor.

"Be thou, oh Hadit, my secret, the Gnostic mystery of my Being, the central point of my connection, my heart itself, and bloom on my fertile lips, made Word!

"Up above, in the infinite heavens, in the profound height of the unknowable, the incessant glow of light is the naked beauty of Nut. She reclines, she bends in delectable ecstasy, to receive the kiss of secret fervor of Hadit. The winged sphere and the blue of the sky are mine.

"O A O Kakof Na Khonsa.

"O A O Kakof Na Khonsa.

"O A O Kakof Na Khonsa."

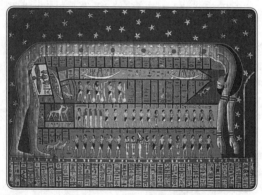

Nut, an Egyptian symbol of the Divine Mother

Invocation of the Divine Mother

"Oh Isis! Mother of the cosmos, root
of love, trunk, bud, leaf, flower and
seed of all that exists; we conjure
Thee, naturalizing force. We call upon
the Queen of space and of the night,
and kissing her loving eyes, drinking
the dew from her lips, breathing
the sweet aroma of her body, we
exclaim: Oh Thou, Nut! Eternal Seity
of heaven, who art the primordial
Soul, who art what was and what
shall be, whose veil no mortal has
lifted, when Thou art beneath the
irradiating stars of the nocturnal
and profound sky of the desert, with
purity of heart and in the flame of
the serpent, we call upon Thee!"

Invocation of the Maiden of Memories

To remember your dreams and experiences
out of your physical body, utilize this prayer.
While in bed, at the time of sleep, invoke your
Inner Being in the following way:

"Father of mine, Thou who art my real Being, I beseech Thee with all of my heart and with all of my soul to take the beloved Maiden of my Memories out from my Ethereal Body, with the goal of not forgetting anything upon returning into my physical body."

Then, while becoming sleepy pronounce the mantras:

"Laaaa Raaaa Sssssss."

It is necessary for the disciple to learn how to take the beloved Maiden of our Memories into his astral travels, in order to bring the memory of all that he sees and hears within the internal worlds. She serves as a mediator between the senses of the physical brain and the ultra-sensible senses of the Astral Body. It comes to be (if the concept fits) that she is like the storage space of memory. To learn more about this practice, see *Esoteric Medicine and Practical Magic* by Samael Aun Weor.

Key of Solomon (Clavis Salomonis)

With this key one can invoke any angel within the physical or astral planes.

"Per Adonai Elohim, Adonai Jehovah, Adonai Sabaoth, Metraton. On Agla, Adonai Mathom, Verbum Pitonicum Misterium Salamandre, Conventum Silphorum, Antragnomorum Demonia Celi, Gad Almousin Gibor, Jeshua Evam Sariatniamic, Veni, Veni, Veni."

"Preserve me, El: for in thee do I put my trust." - Psalm 16:1

Conjurations

To conjure (Latin, cum-jurare; to swear to-gether) is to evoke a superior force in order to reject its opposite or inferior force. To conjure is to make a common act of faith with the invoked force or forces. The greater the strength and enthusiasm of this faith, the more efficacious the conjuration will be.

Conjuration of Jupiter

IAOH, Jovis Pater, IO-Patar (Jupiter the father of all gods) is Christ among the Romans. One can summon his power with the mantras "Te Vigos Cosilim" in order to reject negative forces.

**"In the name of Jupiter,
Father of the gods, I conjure
thee! Te Vigos Cosilim!"**

Conjuration of the Four

This conjuration can be used to cleanse yourself from negative energy; it relates to the four holy creatures mentioned in the Bible (Ezekiel 1), which are the four divine elements of nature: fire (lion), air (eagle), water (angel), and earth (ox).

"Caput mortuum, imperet tibi dominus
    per vivum et devotum serpentem!

"Cherub, imperet tibi Dominus
    per Adam Yod-HaVah!

"Aquila errans, imperet tibi
    Dominus per alas tauri!

"Serpens, imperet tibi
    Dominus Tetragrammaton,
    per Angelum et Leonem!

"Michael, Gabriel, Raphael, Anael!
    Fluat udor per Spiritum Elohim!
    Manet in terra per Adam Yod-HaVah!

"Fiat firmamentum per Yod-
    HaVah-Sabaoth!

"Fiat judicium per ignem
    in virtute Michael!

"Angel of the blind eyes, obey, or
    pass away with this holy water!

"Work winged bull, or revert to the
    earth, unless thou wilt that I should
    pierce thee with this sword!

"Chained eagle, obey my sign,
or fly before this breathing!

"Writhing serpent, crawl at my
feet, or be tortured by the sacred
fire and give way before the
perfumes that I burn in it!

"Water, return to water! Fire, burn!
Air, circulate! Earth, revert to earth!

"By virtue of the Pentagram, which is
the Morning Star, and by the name
of the Tetragram, which is written
in the center of the Cross of Light!

"Amen. Amen. Amen."

The Pentagram, Symbol of the Perfect Human Being

Conjuration of the Seven

This conjuration invokes the seven archangels of creation in order to reject the seven negative planetary psychological crystallizations, whether they are outside of us or within us: lust, anger, pride, greed, envy, laziness, and gluttony.

"In the name of Michael, may Jehovah command thee and drive thee hence, Chavajoth!

"In the name of Gabriel, may Adonai command thee, and drive thee hence, Bael!

"In the name of Raphael, begone before Elial, Samgabiel!

"By Samael Sabaoth, and in the name of Elohim Gibor, get thee hence, Andrameleck!

"By Zachariel and Sachiel-Meleck, be obedient unto Elvah, Sanagabril!

"By the divine and human name of Shaddai, and by the sign of the Pentagram that I hold in my right hand, in the name of the angel Anael, by the power of Adam and Eve,

who are Yod-HaVah, begone Lilith!
Let us rest in peace, Nahemah!

"By the holy Elohim and by the names
of the Genii Cashiel, Sehaltiel, Aphiel
and Zarahiel, at the command of
Orifiel, depart from us Moloch! We
deny thee our children to devour!

"Amen. Amen. Amen."

Conjuration of Gabriel

"Thirteen thousand rays has the Sun,

"Thirteen thousand rays has the Moon,

"Thirteen thousand times may
the enemies I have repent!"

Conjuration in Times of Danger

Samael Aun Weor taught the following magical prayer to be memorized for use in moments of great danger. It is very effective. It is also used as a powerful tool when one needs to penetrate the meaning of a dream or vision.

"Fons Alpha et Omega, Figa, Figalis Sabbaoth, Emmanuel, Adonay, O, Neray, Ela, Ihe, Reutone, Neger, Sahe, Pangeton, Commen, Agla, Matheus, Marcus, Lucas, Johannes, Titulus Triunphalis, Jesus Nazarenus Rex Iudaeorum, Ecce Dominicae Crucis Signum Fugite Partes Adversae, Vicit Leo de Tribu Judae, Radix David Alelluyah, Kyrie Eleison, Christe Eleison, Pater Noster, Ave Maria, et Ne Vos, et Venia Super Nos Salutare Tuum, Oremus."

Royal Conjuration

"I conjure all thy enemies, thy internal
ones as much as thy external
ones, in the portal of Belen.

"I conjure them, and I conjure
them once again, in case they
have a pact with the Devil, black
magic, or backward creeds.

"I conjure them, so that they shall
come humbly to thy feet, as the Lamb
of Christ reached the foot of the Cross.

"I conjure them, so that they shall
come meekly, just as the Lamb came
from the Cross to the eternal Father.

"With two I see them and with three
I fasten them, in the name of the
Father, the Son, and the Holy Spirit."

"Two" represents Mother Nature. "Three" represents the three primary forces.

Prayer for Protection

"Most Holy Mary, pious Mother,
  cover me with your mantle.

"Divine Cross, I ask Thee for
  protection by these three names
  of Jesus, Joachim, and John."

Circle of Protection

When you trace a magical circle around
yourself, whether it is with your sword, with your
willpower and imagination united in vibrating
harmony, or with both at the same time, you
must pronounce the following mantras:

"Helion, Melion, Tetragrammaton."

The magician defends himself against at-
tacks from the demons with the magical circle
and the esoteric pentagram.

Prayer to the Aloe Plant

The elemental (fairy) of the Aloe Vera plant is
beneficial in order to help protect against negative forces. Every Gnostic home should have an
aloe plant. Use this prayer to invoke its assistance.

"Cross, thou art holy and divine.

"Sorcerers and witches
withdraw from this home.

"Such persons, who intend to
arrive here, let it be known
that I am with God.

"Sovereign God, set me free from
treason and from ruination.

"Blessed be the most Holy Mary
and the Consecrated Host."

After you say the prayer, bless the Aloe plant
with the sign of the cross.

Mantra for Protection

Within the astral plane the following mantras form the star of five points with solar light.

"Klim Krishnaya, Govindaya,
Gopijana, Vallabhaya, Swaha!"

To Defeat Demons

"Thou who art the merciful and grandiose Virgin, I beseech Thee, do not allow anything to fall on me. Let me be thy advocate."

In Order to Combat the Demon

"O Divine God!

"I want Thou to help me defeat this demon, that wherever I go Thou shalt help me defeat him.

"I want Thou to protect me from any evil that comes against me.

"Save me from all evilness."

Exorcisms and Healing

To exorcise is to call up or conjure spirits or to chain an isolated spirit. It is important to recite the following exorcisms in Latin (not in English) since Latin is the language that is the most in tune to the forces of nature than any of its derivatives.

Exorcism of the Fire

"Michael, King of the Sun
 and of the Lightning,

"Samael, King of Volcanoes,

"Anael, Prince of the Astral Light,

"I beg Ye to listen to my call. Amen."

Exorcism of the Air

"Spiritus dei ferebatur super aquas,
et inspiravit in faciem hominis,
spiraculum vitae, sit Michael
dux meus, et Sabtabiel servus
meus, in luce et per lucem.

"Fiat verbum halitus meus,
  et imperabo spiritibus aeris
  hujus, et refrenabo equos
  solis voluntate cordis mei,
  et cogitatione mentis meae
  et nutu oculi dextri.

"Exorciso igitur te, creatura
  aeris per Pentagrammaton et
  in nomine Tetragrammaton,
  in quibus sunt voluntas
  firma et fides recta. Amen,
  Sela, Fiat, so be it."

Exorcism of the Water

"Fiat firmamentum in medio aquarum
  et separet aquas ab aquis, quae
  superius sicut quae inferius, et
  quae inferius sicut quae superius ad
  perpetranda miracula rei unius.

"Sol ejus pater est, luna mater et
  ventus hanc gestavit in utero suo,
  ascendit a terra ad coelum et rursus
  a chelo in terram descendit.

"Exorciso te, creatura aquae,
  ut sis mihi speculum del vivi in
  operibus ejus, et fons vitae, et
  ablutio peccatorum. Amen."

Exorcism of the Earth

"By the pole of lodestone that passes
  through the heart of the world, by the
  twelve stones of the Holy City, by the
  seven metals that run inside the veins
  of the earth and in the name of Gob
  obey me, subterranean workers..."

If you are using these exorcisms for healing,
after concluding the Exorcisms of Fire, Air, Water
and Earth, you must pray to your Father, who is
in secret, by saying:

"My Father, my Lord, my God, I set
  myself towards Thee, in the name
  of Adi-Buddha Tetragrammaton.

"Lord of mine, by charity, by Christ,
  Agla, Agla, Agla, I beseech Thee, Ja,
  Ja, Ja, to command my Elemental
  Advocate and this vegetal elemental,
  so that they may place themselves

inside the sick organ of (name the patient) in order to heal him.

"Amen Ra, Amen Ra, Amen Ra."

For Healing the Sick

1. You must first prepare the salt by saying the Exorcism of Salt
2. Place the salt on a metal plate and pour alcohol on top of it
3. Light the mixture and invoke the Cosmic Christ by praying the Gnostic Prayer

Step 1: Exorcism of Salt

"In isto sale sit sapientia, et ab omni corruptione servet mentes nostras et corpora nostra, per Chokmahel et in virtute Ruach-Chokmahel, recedant ab isto fantasmata hylae ut sit sal coelestis, sal terrae et terris salis, ut nutrietur bos triturans et addat spei nostrae cornua tauri volantis. Amen."

The masters of the holy Gnostic Church come to the bedside of the sick person in order to heal them. Every sick person must pronounce this Gnostic Prayer in order to ask the masters for healing.

Step 3: Gnostic Prayer for Healing

"Oh Thou, Solar Logos, igneous Emanation, substance and consciousness of Christ, powerful life whereby everything advances, come unto me and penetrate me, enlighten me, bathe me, go through me, and awaken within my Being all of those ineffable substances that are as much a part of Thee as a part of me.

"Universal and cosmic force, mysterious energy, I conjure Thee, come unto me, remedy my affliction, cure me from this illness and set apart this suffering so that I can have harmony, peace, and health.

"I ask Thee in thy sacred name that the mysteries and the Gnostic Church have taught me, so that Thou can make all of the mysteries of this plane and the superior planes vibrate within me, and that all of those forces together may achieve the miracle of my healing. So be it."

One can also invoke the masters of medicine by chanting the following mantras:

"Antia Da Una Sastaza."

These mantras must be sung when pronounced. After having articulated them, the name of the master one wants to invoke has to be pronounced three times. Sick people can invoke the Master Hippocrates, father of medicine, or Galenus, Paracelsus, Hermes Trismegistus, etc.

Prayer of Our Lady Saint Martha for the Defense of the Body

"O Saint Martha, Thou art blessed, very beloved, and worthy of God, and Thou walk on Mount Tabor.

"Thou entered and encountered the great serpent, then with the Mother of God's girdle Thou tied and bound it.

"Thus, Thou bound the hearts of all my enemies who came against me in the name of the eternal Father and of the Holy Trinity."

Afterwards, pronounce the Apostle's Creed three times.

Apostles' Creed

"I believe in God, the Father almighty,
creator of heaven and earth, and
in Jesus Christ, His only Son, Our
Lord who was conceived by the
Holy Spirit, born of the Virgin Mary,
suffered under Pontius Pilate, was
crucified, died, and was buried.
He descended into hell. The third
day He rose again from the dead.

"He ascended into heaven, and sitteth
at the right hand of God the Father
almighty. From thence He shall come
to judge the living and the dead.

"I believe in the Holy Spirit, the holy
Gnostic Church, the Communion
of Saints, the forgiveness of sins,
the resurrection of the body,
and life everlasting. Amen."

Prayer to Stop Bleeding

"With the blood of Adam, death was born; with the blood of Christ, life was born. Oh blood, stop flowing out!"

Mantras to Heal the Mind

The Mental Body is a material organism that has its own anatomy and physiology. The mantra in order to cure the sicknesses of the Mental Body is:

"S M Hon."

The S is pronounced as a piercing hissing sound, similar to the sound which the brakes of compressed air produce, like this: Ssssssssssssssssssss... The M is pronounced as when one imitates the bellow of the oxen: Mmmmmmmm... The H is like a deep sigh. The syllable ON is pronounced by elongating the sound of the O and the N, like this: OoooooooooNnnnnnnnnnnn...

This mantra must be vocalized daily for one hour. The disciple must invoke daily the Archangel Raphael and Hermes Trismegistus, supplicating them to heal his Mental Body. When the sicknesses of the Mental Body crystallize in the physical brain, then madness is the outcome.

Prayer in Order to Perform Massages and Heal Without Pain

"Jesus, Mary, and Joseph, Most Holy Trinity, the three divine persons. Saint Blas ahead, Saint Peter behind. Saint Blas, if these words are good, then let the tendons and joints return to their place."

Apply the following words in the name of Jesus Christ.

"When Jesus Christ came to the world there were no injuries, no one maimed, no one lame, so let the injuries cease, and Hail, Mary."

Afterwards, pray the "Apostle's Creed" three times. If the injury is not too severe, pray the "Apostle's Creed" three times. However, if the injury is very bad, pray the "Apostle's Creed" nine times. Rub menthol with salt onto the injury.

Invocation of "Mama" Ceferino Maravita for the Healing of Illness Due to Witchcraft

"In the name of Kalusuanga, the primeval god of light, son of the seven red seas and of the seven rays from the Sun, I invoke thee, Mama Ceferino Maravita, so that thou can cure me of my illness. Amen."

One of the most astonishing medic-magicians from the Sierra Nevada of Santa Marta was the Indian Ceferino Maravita. Sick people who suffer from illnesses due to witchcraft must call the "Mama" Ceferino Maravita every night, so that he can cure them from their illness. Recite the above invocation. To learn more about this practice, see *Esoteric Medicine and Practical Magic* by Samael Aun Weor.

Spiritual Practices

Prayer to Attend the Gnostic Church

It is indispensable to take your physical body to the Gnostic Church every Friday and Sunday at dawn in order to receive the Gnostic Holy Unction in flesh and bone. You can also take the physical body from your bed without the need of invoking it from afar. For this, fall asleep while vocalizing the following mantras:

"Miña Pica Frasco."

Then slowly get out of your bed, conserving your slumber. Make a little hop, and if you see yourself inflated and floating, then leave your house and go towards the Gnostic Church.

Prayer in Order to Enchant the Body

When you go to sleep, as you lay under the covers of your bed, pray the following magical prayer thousands of times; when you feel a great deal of drowsiness and a little bit of dreaminess, then get up from your bed while still reciting the prayer. Jump up immediately, fly and travel.

"Philip, Philip, Philip, Apostle
  of our Lord Jesus Christ,
  take me with my body.

"To the little heaven, Philip.

"To the little heaven, Philip.

"To the little heaven, Philip. Amen."

Jinn Prayer

This prayer must be prayed thousands of times in the moments of wanting to sleep. When barely asleep, get up from your bed while still praying and then jump with the intention of floating. If you do not float, go back to bed and repeat the experiment. Have faith.

"I believe in God.

"I believe in my Mother Nature.

"I believe in White Magic.

"My Mother, take me with
  my body. Amen."

Invocation of Samael

While falling asleep, use this invocation to receive assistance in going consciously into the astral plane.

"I believe in God, I believe in Christ, I believe in Samael.

"Samael, take me out of my physical body."

The Archangel Samael as depicted by the Greeks (Ares)

Learn More:
Read *The Divine Science*
by Samael Aun Weor

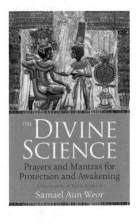

Learn how to protect yourself from black magic, negative forces, witches, sorcerers, and more. Includes techniques for awakening consciousness in the internal worlds, prayers for spiritual defense and healing, and detailed information on how to recognize the influences of black magicians.

978-1-934206-40-9 • $12.95
PAPER • 234 PAGES • 6 x 9 INCHES

Glorian Publishing is a non-profit publisher dedicated to spreading the sacred universal doctrine to suffering humanity. All of our works are made possible by the kindness and generosity of sponsors. If you would like to make a tax-deductible donation, you may send it to the address below, or visit our website for other alternatives. If you would like to sponsor the publication of a book, please contact us at help@ gnosticteachings.org.

Glorian Publishing
PO Box 110225
Brooklyn, NY 11211 US

VISIT US ONLINE AT:
gnosticteachings.org